Deafening as Closing Doors Are

Deafening as Closing Doors Are

The Poetry of Alex Richmond

ALEX RICHMOND

RESOURCE *Publications* • Eugene, Oregon

DEAFENING AS CLOSING DOORS ARE
The Poetry of Alex Richmond

Copyright © 2025 Alex Richmond. All rights reserved. Except for brief quotations in critical publications or reviews, no part of this book may be reproduced in any manner without prior written permission from the publisher. Write: Permissions, Wipf and Stock Publishers, 199 W. 8th Ave., Suite 3, Eugene, OR 97401.

Resource Publications
An Imprint of Wipf and Stock Publishers
199 W. 8th Ave., Suite 3
Eugene, OR 97401

www.wipfandstock.com

PAPERBACK ISBN: 979-8-3852-6054-6
HARDCOVER ISBN: 979-8-3852-6055-3
EBOOK ISBN: 979-8-3852-6056-0

10/30/25

Contents

Two into One | 1
That Said | 2
Happiness | 3
Oh Lazy Till It Happens | 4
Lioness | 5
By Satellite | 6
Insensitive | 7
White Meat | 8
Xerox | 9
A Grievous Injury She | 10
Transient | 11
Thinking About America | 12
Some Photos of Marilyn | 13
Sinatra on YouTube | 14
Thought Crime | 15
The Inheritance | 16
The End of a Friendship | 18
Fame | 19
Unknown | 21
They | 22
Amplitude | 23

Saving | 24
The Decoy | 25
Medals | 26
Anomaly | 27
Smug | 28
Farm Animals | 29
Sheep | 30
The Noblest | 31
New | 32
Tree | 33
Fix | 34
Roy | 35
Pete and the Machine | 36
The Political Interview | 37
The Same Are the Gods | 39
I, Robot | 40
Chrysanthemum | 42
Change | 44
Loot | 45
History | 46
Gold | 47
Diversionary Tactic | 48
By Car | 49
Framing | 50
Old Enough | 51
Living On | 52
Gottfried | 53
The Crocodile | 54
Cool Stations | 55

Micro | 56
Technology | 57
Blenheim Palace Casino | 58
Outside | 59
Société | 60
The Dawn of Film | 61
Being There | 62
The Artist Checks Out | 63
Blue Ocean Scheme | 64
After | 65
The Plan | 66
Raising a Cross | 67
Remembering | 68
Pray on It | 69
Dream of a Bird | 70
Natures No-Mind | 71
Spy | 72
Wife of the Owner | 73

Notes | 75

TWO INTO ONE

They saw the whole of us
Rosy in bone
Or adipose, blown.
Somewhere in time
In the year of the Tiger
In the fact or was it a trap?
They walled us all
In blasted form
Half of each blended,
A visual a ritual trick
Is this what elicits edicts,
Binding forms and nations
Minds and minds?
Indubitably
An ill-advised course.
The time will come,
The community of "nasties"
Seemingly nothing but good denied.
Asked how two could be one.

THAT SAID

That said, I hardly knew it.
The whys and wherefores suspire
To knowledge.
A million dead
And what we think
Only leads to war.

We vanish behind
What people see of us
And speak of the dead
In a universal voice;
It was not me and said
Before I had the time,
Stopping too far, too short.

HAPPINESS

I reiterate I am not great
The satisfactions I feel are miniscule and pure,
Don't invalidate me with a large image.
In our world happiness is performed
Or is the quest for something large
Or is the measure of love.
I cannot say I have money,
I am not for your greater delectation
A manifestation in physical form.
I slide away but stay in the memory
(All the while fading).
I am sunlight in its yellow conflagrations,
I am partial freedom, I am large in symbol
And I suspend time like a stare or a star.

OH LAZY TILL IT HAPPENS

Oh lazy till it happens, tell me you didn't
know it can change you thought summer
could last forever.
Glimmer like the wall of shiny cards, the twin houses
reflect everything going on downtown.
Stand like you are strong until it's too
close to say whether fame is a reflection
of something or the structure.
What if the structure's wrong?
What if fame hides a towering infirmity
and you share your DNA with your twin?
Oh lazy till it happens, we thought
summer would go on and on perhaps
we knew they were coming for us.
In the American city
nothing glitters for long but is
put up again by its stupid sister
and time will keep on hating
anything bigger and better,
so anything that glitters is a sin.

LIONESS

Returning to the shock of you,
Paused by your door you're smaller,
And time has made an art of you,
Made the most of your natural precision.
I remember you larger, warmer;
They are an anathema to a capable lioness
Who would not let a man hunt her.

Returning elevates us,
Not knowing elevates us
To see how we were when lioness and loneliness met.
What of us?
This study in loving stands as a testament,
Hanging-out with time but moving further back,
Or filed under half ruined, half diminished
"We never knew what she saw in him."
But as time finishes it by folding blackly over it,
I sleep dreaming we are dancing afresh.

Standing at your door watching something in nature,
Studying you lioness.

BY SATELLITE

You are not real;
There is a point at which you become real

It's called love.
You were dying unselfconsciously,

I ignored you.
They may have asked for funds (for water)

I couldn't tell you.
Something told me not to care,

Came between us.
You and me here and there

Could never reach.
TV anesthetizes the vision

And at a distance
You are untruthful just a picture

And we can't love.
This is TV as voyeurism.

But the satellite
That sends me the artifact

Has missed. Allowed
Your eye to contact mine softly.

Why does true love confound
Even satellites?

INSENSITIVE

Sold out to Pinscher
In Friedrichshafen,
He crouches with his sow
Some wife or façade,
Flame, amour, tryst,
Splits doubloons in a yard . . .
A lazy sea, eventualities,
Far out.
The same enthroned half-wit
Harkens powers.

WHITE MEAT

What Shankaracharya might have meditated
the labyrinth of binary—
cold tools to excavate a nerveless brain.
When truth is not whole
the composite of schmuck from which we come,
the tower of the mind would invent a puppeteer
and its joke—a carcass, a dead cow.
What is a life reduced to specks?
Impossible choices,
better and better photography.

XEROX

Oh sad you,
Took the place of a stereotype
They will slide after you
(Noting they envelope all regions
And come to nothing).
Curling replica-like
Slide beneath all mankind
Dirtying the eye. Swastikas.

A GRIEVOUS INJURY SHE

Such a grievous injury she,
A passionate material.
Had hoped
(the start of a nuclear winter)
Love could mitigate biology
And the spun sugar neuron
(Black as rat's chances now and damned).
I knew to hope (isn't that the point?)
And love such a difficile material.

TRANSIENT

Saints preserve we are small
Cradled and swaddled
What held all these years
Hosannas, prayers, hopes?

The story mirrors
All life's defeats;
The money
The lovers, friends,
Reading the same reverse book.
Must be right—just nod
That "above" is something else.
Mothers are blamed.

THINKING ABOUT AMERICA

These are ocean gates.
Beyond them swells the blood of America
Freezing-out the morning tide with its silven nature.
True America rests upon the sublimation of the self,
Enough to ensure clear vision.

The ocean is a spirit-mask
Suspended over plains and patterned eyots.
A tangential mirror,
Invalidating human behavior at the point of elation,
Burnishing the "silver-dollar" states with its warm panache.

Hopper's painted tenements are partially sunlit
Reflect "small-time" America,
Frank Lloyd won tributes softly merging
Wood, glass, and brick.

Naturally an expansion of American thought.

Lovers are lost here,
Turn to stone or amorphize into vaunted scenery.
Technicolor will fade out, but the films the lakes make
Show Gooney birds, pines, and a white con-trail.

        If you stop here you bring

Medicinal cliché, iodine smiles.
The curious ability to limit pain
Is a reflection of the scenery.
We can talk about how we have grown,
But we are small against nature.

SOME PHOTOS OF MARILYN

The hopeless weight of a dove falling
Perhaps this comes to mind,
Or the way once wrought, photos
Gain weight and fall in time;
Heavier naturally than falling trees.

For a while I hear Marilyn
And she fades, but the whole mistake
Is that she doesn't go, is thinking
That she's alive and merely late,
Not frigid in the peripatetic sea.

We may half know her but half best
Will not avert the fall;
Without linking the weight with the flesh,
Will not recover or restore
Marilyn; the trivial guise

The promiscuity, the real personality
Is not what you think you know;
The fabulous insecurity the "Kennedys"
Putting on make-up before a show,
"Chanel 5" atomized

Twinkles in the dark for eternity.
The alter ego, the winking eye . . .
All you can say with certainty
Is that death should have weight
Let a fallen dove lie.

SINATRA ON YOUTUBE

Watching a black-and-white film of your life,
Stepping out of a car onto a wet pavement—
You killed a radio reporter with a look,
Hurried past a theater façade
To the entrance under a vertical alphabet.
The portrayal has you silkily sketched
The real Sinatra
Is the man we mistook
For a passer by then hooped in amazement
At the thought of you come alive.
And that you're not Sinatra you're a real man,
Is an image that's hard to create.
Real lovers evolve and die, we have a clock
That measures our reality.
But this film of you stopped in '55
And you're trapped on my hard drive.
It's a fact of humanity
To continuously evolve
But your destiny is to be late.
A sad thing for such a punctual man.

THOUGHT CRIME

A fly on it.
wasn't seen before nor is it a sign of summer
switching its way this way and that,
instinctively something is wrong at the top
"all the perfumes of Arabia will not sweeten . . ."
A fly on it, what was pure
or at least our instinct and was reasonable,
splits the view into a hundred each
and each a lower version . . .
A fly on it
might mean a switch in perspectives
or a hundred versions of the truth
or a hundred prejudices
we should be careful.

THE INHERITANCE

What comes after;
Refreshing, renewing,
Or an argument?
You say we keep it the same
For the sake of memory,
Invoke a pause a photo;
A long angle through a lens—
The two of them together at the end
Frozen out.

Nowhere now except
The way the sun projects
On the kitchen wall.
And this is "living on"
From memory and from love
And so do we become

The inseparable brothers
Slumming together,
Lazy around a stump,
At the signs of death
Carnivorous in the miles of jagged country?

I had been thinking about why
It was better
And why we let them die
And lied by knowing.
That they stayed together
And we . . .

Obeyed the time-honored code
Of families;
That there is strength in adversity
Neither love nor the absence of it.

THE END OF A FRIENDSHIP

Fought our bodies here
(I knew it was you when the door creaked,
You entered with the wind).

We sat and it came to pass;
The arguing shadows,
The evening light,

Found us on neutral ground,
Accepting accolades—
"Tolerance Beyond Duty"

And high time, old friend!
I heard the fizzing, lit a fuse
The day we met in idealism.

Warm days, arm in perilous arm,
The people we enthrone
We let die.

Remember the love?
The point of our interdependency,
Motifs, signs,

Beautifully ignored,
By all of the hopeless lovers.

FAME

Summer at the farm,
what it is to be famous a second in and at the margin;
cities, multitudes . . .

For a day to encapsulate a life they slow time
and what speed a minute or a second?

A ball dances on top of a fountain.

We are cherished by them, and are part of them, and yet
It is the luck of the Irish not to be stained,
If they took pictures in "earth years,"
They and only they would perish.

On the farm they neither sleep nor dream,
The eye possesses the moment
then it is resubmitted.
They will succumb to age,
to dangerous stuff with a radium half-life.

From a social perspective they need us
As we need them but majesty suspends;
the cars twinkle, the sun burns out the blue,
dirty dusty streets, arguments in cafes,
a busker thumps a tin,
the Queen stirrups a horse in the palace garden.

"To be famous is to suspend reality, agree or disagree?"

Summer at the farm, the perpetual weekend,
the end and the beginning,
what it is to others imaginatively
"they" can be.

They suspend the beginning and the end.

(Preening themselves in ecstasy)

A red button printed: "Press to be Free"
would we ever,
and in a second, they are a living photograph,
And they are what we see.

UNKNOWN

Came in and left miraculously,
Something you "gave" (yourself)
Unnoticed.
God is glad perhaps,
And life (the "undefinable"
—we cannot think beyond the self)
Is saved again; it is sad,
(though in defiance of the suggestion).
You came with your worth
And added some measure unknown.

THEY

They walk in dust, they say they are dry,
Invincibility hurts from the Mafia to Mao Zedong.

The hearts' joy, its pink knot
Plasticized.

Tries to be like the wind ventilating, forgetting . . .

They suffer as they slide, the desert scorched
Conveys some rough thought-form polyglot,

More the sin than the sinning
The porosity of gods.

AMPLITUDE

Stay "home" they have you for a leper
The game at the end of the rainbow
Is to be all and one,
Chalk this up in simple crayon, push on.

All corners are a military to might
And from here so small
As to be indistinguishable,
A note of light aimed for infinity.

To all a sense of place.

SAVING

Piling up behind the door
You keep resolutely shut,
what wonders would have been?
It is sweeter to feign disillusion,
and fear has grown fat
on too much given.
As if life were for the taking,
once and for all and nothing left.
You save and keep on saving.

THE DECOY

Sing sing, for that thing
Always lies, what you know
Is the route to the thing
Or the story or the telling
Or some such rhyme;
Sing sing for nothing,
Nothing is in it, what you show
Is what you win
For a simple act of rebellion,
There's no such crime.

MEDALS

Your medal defines you,
Runs rings around you.
Now you're all tied up in ribbons,
So what are you if not hidden?

ANOMALY

The silver taps
Wriggle a reflection,
Who in the world would call it a day?
The force that rails against nature
Reaches in with intimate precision
Minds to play,
The pill and the cause.
A million infinitesimals
Each innocent.

SMUG

Smug is as smug does,
Nothing unusual,
The guest that blessed
A thousand principles
Pirouetted on the principle
Invincible, I guessed
That is the hole you dug,
I handed you the spade.

FARM ANIMALS

An unfair creation,
They took a seed that grew
In exploitation; lame mares,
Mutilated sheep, mad cows,
Cattle for beef
Isn't that beyond belief?
If you are a sow you experience
Oneness with nature
Its ingredients indigestible
For town spirits
But your stock and want.
If it is fair, in recognition
Of our need
We think we deserve to eat
Mere pig, but why not
Live and let live?

SHEEP

They hate nothing, summer brings
Sleep and mother what you may
Say is "poor sheep" mindful of
Murder for what we think we need.
You might say something—words scatter
As words are blind to sheep.
Summer sings. "We" are not certain.
This is the start and the end of infinity.

THE NOBLEST

Dumb pervs brought up to believe
We're the best things living, that
Somehow, our words
Confer nobility that's silly.
Years later I know this.
Wondering what it's about
Fears awaken
And all in a tangle I doubt.
Our world isn't conveyed
By gods gracious giving,
For us at least forgiving.
Forgetting to live simplistically
Is more our fate
That nature doubts our efficacy
And gambles that "it" will out.

NEW

Glowing, she will not apologize
For bringing "it" in.
It's an Olympic ride
And just in time,
Coming is better than going and
To shine like they do and with pride
And something you and you and you
Know; it might be the first
It shan't be the last.
So simple there is no need
To apologize, that is;
When Eileithyia spoke she
Meant it like this.
A tender moment
To shape love and who knows
Down the road?

TREE

She made a shape you can't argue with
And she's made like a tree,
And your elaborate plan won't match
Her elaborate plan to spread and stay.
As if coming is a long way
And is a long way going
And is a long time dead.
She annotates branches that
Say how to be free
And how to stand,
And what is to be said.
Say nothing,
Words bend.

FIX

It's smug to know everything is right
And evil is untried, it ties you to a game,
Evil speaks and evil denies.
Smile for the sake of the newborn,
Smile for the sake of the game,
When you came in shouting
"Love shan't be denied"
Didn't they warn
With a panoply of horns?

ROY

Turn around for Roy,
He's the past shooting towards us,
Always zooming round corners,
Never quite in the eye for long enough.
I think he's a nuisance a ploy.

Turn around for Roy,
See him in his flaming Canopus
Claiming he'll make a man of us,
Rip roaring "Boys Own" stuff.
But seemingly, fleetingly, annoys.

Spot him in the clouds: Roy,
At the speed of sound in the jet age,
Soaring over a summer parade,
Or split like an atom over Bikini Bay.
Oh! Boys will be boys!

Turn around for Roy,
He's almost past his sell-by date
And by some concomitance of fates
We turn and meet him face-to-face.
The man before the boy?

PETE AND THE MACHINE

Pete is idle or is stressed, no in-between,
And his weakness is he's acquiesced;
Unlike a machine—it shudders at such idleness.

Pete can think about what he sees,
Can turn his mind 180 degrees,
And express love—THIS BIG!—
Hate, and of course irony.

The machine yearns "not" to be free
Precisely to avoid such incomprehension,
Who needs freedom when you can be an engine?

Who needs a mind
When a mind renders you senseless
To violence and genocide?
And psychiatry can't mend you.

THE POLITICAL INTERVIEW

Time has propelled a question, always a question.
Andrew Marr* in tailored suit "untethered."
Try to imagine an answer to end all of this
Try to imagine . . . the intimate dissection
To tiny pieces painstakingly put together,
The tremendous hardness of an iron fist.

Dust on the floor is blown in arteries, seeping
Behind eyes, grinds under patent polished shoes,
A door closes with a crash, "imagine you had the cash . . .
What would you do?" Try to relieve
Yourself of pain, try and pick and choose
The answer to a question, attempt a splash.

The tawdry tabloids always have it neat
Promote a harsh "know-it-all" perspective;
They should try to run it all, secular,
Ungodly, never what you would wish to meet
On any orderly night. Marr is selective,
Proposes a thing or two, makes you look avuncular,

Idiot even, though more harrowed than idiot,
Hammered into corners that just won't fit,
Right and wrong are interchangeable in the end,
Interwoven. "I felt I was Judas Iscariot
Invariably the man who lets you down, I wish
I was one upon whom you depend."

Strike a pose, take a stand, not just streams
Of dust writhing under and over you, Mr. Marr,
Or is this what it is to be politic?

The seasonal bluff not the stuff of dreams;
To be remembered as the man who took apart
The truth or learnt how to twist it.

*Andrew Marr is a British political journalist.

THE SAME ARE THE GODS

The same are the gods
Ruminating on our blood,
Not telling us what we are here for
It must be something,
But smaller for the knowing?
Smaller because blood is like wine
For sharks for gods.
The purer thing
It should be for not telling
Is a serial lapse;
The first hand cradled in a hand,
The warmth of a loving body
Should rend spirit apart
Though cannot say who we are.
Something in linear time,
The product of money
Or how the market works,
Building prosperity for the few.
Ah, the gods and the sharks cruise and slide!
Artful in metempsychosis
Careful to minimize
What is known;
Dummy code (0's and 1's),
Or for gods "dial a hero."
The lack of meaning has its purposes.
The same are the gods,
Their similar vices,
Their lust for blood,
Their willingness to hide,
Are ours.

I, ROBOT

Did you feel the earth move
A sense of matter re-forming?
The breathing of pure logic

Will soon be a part of you,
Is something more evolved
Than Einstein (gay fantasy object!)

Did you feel the earth tilt,
Imperceptibly, unexpectedly rock?
I am a common man and understand

The way democracies are built,
The primacy of the mob.
I too am from primordial silt sand

And like you implore logic
And know that it fits,
And we're all fools and life goes on.

Do you believe we are tragic,
Or living in connubial bliss
Fruitfully a million summers long?

I remembered a sea, an old sun,
A lover. Do you believe in time,
That age is what makes us?

The mechanism is steely tough,
Subterranean, subhuman grime
Implores us to rise up.

Love, drugs, the preachers
May ameliorate;
Sex, stupid fucks, the game

May amuse us, and science
(The ultimate explanation)
Will imbue us with the same

Sets of feelings, the same dust;
Disposed to play along,
Evolve mechanical bureaucracies.

Seas, setting suns, vistas,
Are blameless, they react
With virginal clarity,

Nothing is beneath us,
We reduce to facts,
This is reality.

The tide draws a neat
Veil, magnifies sand
Stirring electric fish.

The word on the street
Is change, sciences' plan,
I hope will make us fit.

CHRYSANTHEMUM

What is it
The scent of a Chrysanthemum,
The Chrysanthemum of a past life?
The comfort of flowers for a child, for the elderly
Extrapolates the past.

The Chrysanthemum is heat
Is the scent of heat
Heat of summers stranger than love,
Yes, darker even than love.

Advancing lovers burst into worlds
With the scent of Chrysanths
The petal pit densely pressed
The scent of youth.
But with age
The grind of matter and antimatter,
The vase doomed on the watery sill.

Oh those Chrysanths take me back
To summers never ending,
When the nearest garden stood impossibly still
And we dug so as to uncover a sin or a song:

"Oh my tenement love, oh my tenement love
That's my type of love
In '42 the elemental glue
That binds me to you
Is the scent of Chrysanthemum."

Bombs came in summer '42
And individual Chrysanths burst forward in eternity.

We hope that words will bring us closer or music,
But hope secretly to be alone with fragrance.

CHANGE

The urge is to hang on after the moment
With a kind of delicious awe,
The careful climb
To another moment
Is a posture in the raw,
A citation for the clock,
The clock as law.

It's curious, but hope (so often a hopeless state)
Is the way of you;
Sent on against a restless god (a forlorn god),
Sent on against fate
Through a banshee wood,
Love is a ramshackle essence,
And love hoped for is rarely good.

What I could say is that it can't end
But that's not the rule
It brims along
Through infinite bends
Indicating that me and you
Are like water,
Slipping and sliding abating rules.

Perhaps we can let go kindly (or at least slowly),
If we let go at all.
Though the "signs"
Are that we hoped
Too high and that we "will" fall
To a perfunctory stop
Swept up on a new shore.

LOOT

He stoops to bank, summons strength to pay bills,
A path runs in his head from the void of intellect
From pasts long dead when he had to stoop to kill or be killed.

Discusses what truths are—whores to a nomadic tribe,
Nods congenially smiles
With a smile half what's meant love or embellishment?
All love is dark, all truths hidden,
Distributed in the wind.

All bum paths and bum steers are born of fear
Of speaking truth to keep our own form or our idiocy near.
We all walk up this path,
Or the other, and fail through kindness.
For death views death indifferently and its orchestras are stars.

He reaches to grasp the eternal sun
Half-blinded, half-enraged,
He reaches to grasp an eternal love,
Or anything large,
It's what he does.
He lives to grasp—love, money, irresolution.

The communion of saints fall
Like a crashing orchestra, scatter oaths
About the love and money
And how good it is to save (so we don't run out before the end),
Muttered truths about surety.
That only God is truth

And distributes it thin
In a homeopathic solution.

HISTORY

It's history the devilish thing,
The space between the beating wings
Disturbs the air in dusty arcs.
It's a paean to impropriety
The death of almost everything.

Time folds like a blackened star
Its deception is its complete dispersal;
Self-gassing and poisoning
After a bright era of sensuality.
And what do you care
If we lose our meaning, the simplistic way
Is making equality
—the barking dog—
And how can you feel what beauty is when
All you can say is "it wasn't"
And "time won't tell"?
The space between the beating wings,
The poetry of air,
Is all that time crafted.

GOLD

The myth is told (all rich men know,
past lives damned in hell)
In whispers (close cousins of death)
And the bitch could never a lover be.
Let's pretend;

For what is it
But happy happenstance?
That is to show for a life a golden lot
And know a sham as a sham.
Mining for gold digs an equal
Amount out of you,
You can't put it back,
It forever adorns.

DIVERSIONARY TACTIC

My golden knowledge, my feat,
Has a faded antiquarian air;
We're always chasing the past, facing its charm
In an irreconcilable mirror.
Moves me to tears
The strength needed to move from era to era.
Might be unkind, but dovetails are for the weak,
Snap in reality any sensitive truth
So better secure it,
Envision it strong in the flush of youth;
Past, present, future the beautiful trick,
Are certainly not true but take you in their grip.
While phenomena's unwind which do I pick?

BY CAR

This is where it's all happening
Where the movement is, the gist,
Where the living live
Each encapsulated
And flash by fast.
Are a metaphor if nothing is
For what we are; poor, poor by
Happening by being by far.
The less connected of the animals
By car.

FRAMING

That's "the nothing" sausage
The world that exists on air
Then forgotten.
"Next please."
Some "stick," that's history—
A single-cell organism
And nothing deep.
Do you care?
The curve of the world is surface
Not forgiven freedoms,
Watch and listen.

OLD ENOUGH

Oh you didn't ask to be formed
with all that accompanies it;
anger, hate, psychopathy, sex,
the oddments of the season . . .
And struggling into a skirt
too small to be good for anything
more or less.
Altercating verbally, bodily,
until you can control it.
Veering off at a tangent will
be compensated by
learning to fit the system.
Is this what you wanted?
You didn't ask to be born,
to interject with your flesh,
held up as a reason for equality.
It is no wonder these things
are of no interest, you have
nothing to invest beyond the law.

LIVING ON

Sitting there comfortably
And every hour is "after hours."
What could it be
When you are so loved
That took you for a mishap
And troubled your "troubles,"
And sent you recompense (flowers)?

GOTTFRIED

Gottfried made "a way,"
Made a link for always,
And you ask him
Which way is "the way."
Ask Gottfried if he prays,
Ask if God lives
Ask if God stays,
Keep on guessing
Which way?

THE CROCODILE

Blessed with knowing little, only texture
and with inner vision,
we settle to watch a biopic—the story of our lives.
No linear thing measures how far we are and the swamp
reimagines, reflects sun and sky.
Photographed no doubt talked about
but the sum of our fears?
And the crocodile loves plainly dainty feet,
don't blame it; all things measured in truth
pass by a circuitous route.
The diametric mark, the scar, mention freedom.
Or any denizen of the deep, the white shark
or the purity you see
if you are a rat
and the epitome of your function.
Travel with a sense of ease; tooth and comb set,
black bowler hat, a stranger in the strange land.
You think you "Know It All"
save for the "art," the beginning and the end.

COOL STATIONS

White farms pass on the train to Rome,
Vacant winds blow
Paper fixtures in loose curls.
Ascend and face a firm
Heat, a fiery blast
Fades the iconoclast.
In a valley a stone river flows.

Kingdom of sun, a burlesque!
Try white linen to redress
A loving warmth; a tired sore
Logic harms the wonder of it all.
It never lasts,
Though if we're fast,
The tricks of light we collect.

Cool stations line the heated way
And turns reveal a blustered bay
As façade; the imagination
Frames a tottering nation.
Abate the normal glance,
Plunge unhindered on a chance—
The art of the child at play.

Give me the sun, the honey blest,
The heart's too warm to obsess;
A million sorrowful ways await
The mind apprehensive of its fate.
An open heart
A sun to charm,
Is the sum of our interest.

MICRO

Micro, too complete and knows
That smallest is not least.
If big mind had small components
What in the world would grow?
Unquestionably from the seed.
Micro is God, unknown
For a series of divided moments;
Binary bit code not blind control?

TECHNOLOGY

I'm ascending technology boldly,
You either love it or hate it but I prefer
To hope it will help me, if I side with it
(so near I can hear it purr) it might not bite me.

I'm defending technology as though
Someone had put me at ease,
Hoping the conversation will set me free, yes I like it
(gliding my hand over its fur) in spite of me.

When I touch it I sense a thrill
An expectation it can hardly contend
And which I allow and upon which I come to depend
Puts me precariously in its power.
Who wants to make an enemy of technology?

I have a list of criteria it should fulfill
Although they won't be tested.
Who questions the power of the epoch when it's electric?
Who climbs "half way" up a tower?
When I get to the top I will jump off symbolically.

BLENHEIM PALACE CASINO

We're down for the weekend to take a break,
Invent some wheeze and Jeeves will ensure
We're topped up.

Some would say it's an unmitigated act of rape
That such a stately place should implore
The likes of us,

But it made economic sense, English Heritage
And the government are planning a thousand
Accessible by bus.

It now means that we preserve a vestige
Of England's splendor—old-fashioned
By any other name.

Put a penny in the slot, hose down, freshen.
Do the things you wanted to but never could,
Don't be a schmuck!

It's all here for the taking now, could be heaven,
And those old bores who built it would
Be thunderstruck.

It really means a lot, to preserve the order
Of things without the platitudes
To spoil the fun.

The palace chapel is now a sauna,
Unisex, mirrored to strike the mood.
Though it's substantially the same.

OUTSIDE

Sat outside
A span of a life its brave bright light
Will warm us to its concept,
Drop the head anoint in the name of the Christ.

Each brought in at the start of a clock,
Each cellular light indicates we live separately
Although try to connect.

Lovers span the dark and dance under the moon,
Only love can shape the truth,
And is what we all take with us
From death into life, life into death.

Sat outside
A span of life in infinite space is a kind of freedom,
But lovers know the beauty of life at its best.
Only lovers connect with life and with death.

SOCIÉTÉ

Shall I illumine, for my sins . . .
Why and why not?
The reason is behind silly glass
Laughing at folk,
Distorting belief, no wonder
Drugs bring some alignment.
You have to meet silly with silly
To achieve visibility.

THE DAWN OF FILM

Smells of '29, oh I could cry and cry,
The scenes that I hoped would live twice
Are bluesy and un-unified.
They won't separate from the march of time;
Dusty clichés "Noddy" cars pianos etching rhymes
All denote the formula of the era.

Smells of '29, no matter how hard I try
I can't remember the truth so I lie,
It's in the minds' eye, the way we were.
Not being the intellectual kind what I know
Is personal bravura, and hardly well-defined;
Like Garbo you can't get any nearer.

BEING THERE

Being there.
Historians can only dream
But what they see is magic,
And what they work is
Unique and new and unfair.
It had for others served its purpose
And burned in the rhythmic air;
Each have had their view from "now,"
Wished they could blink back
To something heroically completed.
But you can't reverse a world.
And if happiness is a second
Or a fraction of a second
And the rest annihilation,
That force escapes the atom.
Oh! And what comes next?
We're taught that the world is a series
Of likely events (science)
And that life traps fact.

THE ARTIST CHECKS OUT

Let us go lightly, be wise around it.
Describing its distance makes it exotic
like a filmic scene,
but to be close is too modern too mean.
Extend a molecular probe
while gravity creaks
or expel parachutes with tiny men in tiny seats.
Let us go, let us go
but softly, at a distance,
too close breaks it down into component parts.
(If you look too hard
you see into the bowels of hell.)
Peer inside with a monocle
but not so close that something goes awry.
Don't breach an interior scene
and its attendant sweaty fumblings.
This is where Nazism is.
Sometimes I graze a gossamer wing
succumb to that tribal thing,
though I am generally invincible
and have no compunction to love.
The reverse quite the reverse.
The strength of you is as a team
and you don't have selfish dreams
Though you're too hurt to dream individually.

BLUE OCEAN SCHEME

Those who dive
Slip away plastic, frayed
Telescopic net
Spectral like Cathedral
At depth.
Hardly self-contained.
We plumb and stretch to
Mariana Trench and Space
And rubbish death.

AFTER

What was left of it
Seemed long.
What could have been,
In code or is it a cosmic trick
I am stuck not to have known.
Before the ways and wherefores
The evening walk around the gods;
We stopped and kissed
Thinking we could remit
And forgetting we are original,
We must individually roar.

Scattered the Doves.
Sunk the ship.

THE PLAN

You can't ban, the plan bans,
Stands the same old rights
Hand on hand,
And it will ~~fight~~ guide
A level of pain, apply
Tight the blame—am I right?

RAISING A CROSS

Down in the earthbed of suburbia
Sometimes curses are cash and worse
TV is King and sometimes
Spending is a way to heaven.

Sown in the coldbed,
Consummate flowers
Proclaim dated laws.
Matrimony and remuneration
Are a way of
Cussing or sweating for an idea of heaven

(askew dimension, dimension without union)

So we raise a cross of love
Curse its rough wood
Its deadweight its raw dimension,
Here in suburbia harassed by its message.

And what do we do
In an age of reason
To radiate the spirit,
Rejuvenate the soul?
No act of reason enough
Or balletic enough.

(nothing of consequence or dimension or union)

REMEMBERING

The seeds of them,
A dirty sun fans a distant view.

The seeds of them stick in the parietal eye and stem,
Attend small rows of houses chalk white in the afternoons.

Nocturnally cleanse these days from new,
Brash, unkempt.
The seeds of them
Glitter on mixed in the spoil at Glynea
Filter through years; no ego or sub-sperm dumb by necessity,
Know too late they have proselytized purity,
Should be mad like beauty.
The seeds of them in rays of sun symbolize continuity.

PRAY ON IT

Pray on it
Is this laziness?
Pray on it
Walk away.

An explosion an expatriation
Of body parts a bomb in Iraq
Is an offence to the sense
So I pray a while.

Pray on it
To end all the pain,
Pray on it
And walk away.

The feeble attempt is artfully meant,
Secures a place in the human race,
Somehow registers magically
Sympathy, empathy.

DREAM OF A BIRD

Woken by a bird but unable to be that
I turn twisting sheets sunshine blind.
The bird takes the plaudit
Igniting flame and feather.
I return to dreaming:

"A chateau, a pattern of fountains
(a bird would see as 'abstract' beauty),
Cutting above with a folded twig."

Anonymous vistas are all we need;
You ask me what a dream can be
Far less than a bird.
Wake up wake up!
Was it something I heard?

NATURES NO-MIND

Natures no-mind.
Feathers ruffle in the breeze,
Blue sky is seen within a pattern of branches.

All are of no mind and no mind is so composed so comforted,
No equanimity is so like the equanimity of the kill
Automatic and un-sinning and unrepentant.

The eagle's sparkling eye is as elegant as a life for a life.

Natures no-mind isn't dumb it is the explanation in poetry
The human brain has skipped because its thinking divides
Good from bad, right from wrong, and makes it all fit
Believing the higher things.

We yearn for moral verification in centimeters
Because we must measure relative values.
But in the end all values and kindnesses have no verification,
And all thinking shouldn't exist:

We may atone for the sins of thinking.

SPY

Define incognito?
Photoreceptors stirring,
wooden houses black with ice at Varangerbotn,
the beards of old men
black with wine.
Define, define the life of a spy,
halfway to the casino,
on the coast road to Monte Carlo.
The hope is to be recognized,
what else to hope when you are blind?
Define incognito or do you pursue
a special connection to it
a predilection for fog
or "faux fog"?
A spy hurts for definition
and posits to himself he has none.
That's the point,
the absence of something has shape
is hard to disguise.
You call yourself a spy?

WIFE OF THE OWNER

Pretty but teeth missing,
Whippety as her dog,
Things not looked after
Suffer under God.
Silly, wishy-washy,
Wishing for "Mr. Nice."
Will crack a smile, half in denial.
Half a woman, too soon tied
To the party balloon, life.
Undeniably my type,
Had she not been his wife,
Had she not been his wife.

Notes

TWO INTO ONE
How ideologies can pollute the mind and the spirit.

INSENSITIVE
Could be "I was ripped off by my business partner."

WHITE MEAT
Myopia. The Digital Age.

XEROX
The same as above.

THEY
We are not who we purport to be. Purity is perhaps desirable but unobtainable.

AMPLITUDE
Utopias and "The Singularity" as developed by Kurzweil is probably not good.

NOTES

I, ROBOT

The technocratic age. The robot forewarns us about the changes taking place and boasts that we are similar.

CHRYSANTHEMUM

Chrysanthemums have less fragrance than I thought. But they have some. Exploring the idea of memory and fragrance.

HISTORY

We work so hard to improve, but it is as nought; this is the conundrum of epochs. In so doing, we often ignore the good things of the past, the beauty and art, the sense of meaning brought by literature and the devotional texts. Ultimately the past fades, as does the present, and people are bound by similar limitations throughout time.

OLD ENOUGH

Vulnerability can be exploited.

LIVING ON

Medical care for the elderly that disables. Not being allowed to grow old gracefully.

GOTTFRIED

God freed. Has a dual meaning. Gottfried is a German Christian name meaning "Peace of God."

THE CROCODILE

We think we know it all. Don't be scared. If it eats you, it is only natural.

MICRO
The Digital Age.

BLENHEIM PALACE CASINO
Repurposing important historic buildings to make them pay for themselves. This is, of course, exaggerated but who knows?

THE ARTIST CHECKS OUT
The poor artist doesn't fit in.

REMEMBERING
The past should be allowed to grow in us. This is about nostalgia and how a particular community from the past is remembered or forgotten, as the case may be. I propose that life was simpler and more in line with natural law. Glynea is a mining town, and the past is thrown away / buried deep. Modern life seems equitable and clean but is brash and dirty. We ignore the past thinking that modernity offers everything good, but it doesn't always deliver.

NATURES NO-MIND
Unthinking nature is free in the truest sense. Our ability to think can imprison us, and the infinite choice thinking provides causes us to harm nature and ourselves.

WIFE OF THE OWNER
Owner of the wife.